# Contents

## Sailing the seas

Mighty wooden ships explored the seas

during the Golden Age of Piracy (1690–1730).

Pirates worked hard to look after

their ships. They always had

to be ready for the next raid.

by Rosalyn Tucker

Consulting editor: Gail Saunders-Smith, PhD

Raintree is an imprint of Capstone Global Library Limited, a company incorporated in England and Wales having its registered office at 7 Pilgrim Street, London, EC4V 6LB – Registered company number: 6695582

www.raintree.co.uk
myorders@raintree.co.uk

**Editorial Credits**
Michelle Hasselius, editor; Kazuko Collins, designer; Pam Mitsakos, media researcher; Gene Bentdahl, production specialist

ISBN 978 1 406 29352 4 (hardback)
19 18 17 16 15
10 9 8 7 6 5 4 3 2 1

ISBN 978 1 406 29357 9 (paperback)
20 19 18 17 16
10 9 8 7 6 5 4 3 2 1

**British Library Cataloguing in Publication Data**
A full catalogue record for this book is available from the British Library.

**Photo Credits**
Alamy: © ClassicStock, 9, © PARIS PIERCE, 13; Bridgeman Images: Peter Newark Historical Pictures, 5; Dreamstime: © Gordan, 17; Mary Evans Picture Library, 11; Newscom: ZUMA Press/Jon Mitchell, 21; Shutterstock: Denis Tabler, 15, Elenarts, cover; Superstock, 7, 19
Design Elements: Shutterstock: A-R-T (old paper), La Gorda (rope illustration), vovan (old wood)

Every effort has been made to contact copyright holders of material reproduced in this book. Any omissions will be rectified in subsequent printings if notice is given to the publisher.

All the internet addresses (URLs) given in this book were valid at the time of going to press. However, due to the dynamic nature of the internet, some addresses may have changed, or sites may have changed or ceased to exist since publication. While the author and publisher regret any inconvenience this may cause readers, no responsibility for any such changes can be accepted by either the author or the publisher.

Printed in China.

Many sailors feared pirate attacks at sea.

Pirates often stole ships.
But pirate ships needed to
be fast. So pirates made the
ships lighter. The lighter
the ship, the faster it sailed.

After winning a battle, pirates often stole the ship and the treasures on board.

## Ship sizes

Small, fast ships made good pirate ships. These ships could easily sneak up on others and attack. Small ships could also hide in shallow waters.

Many pirates sailed on small ships called schooners.

A few pirates sailed on large, heavy warships. The warships could not move or turn as quickly as small ships. But large ships could carry more weapons and treasures.

Black Bart sailed one of the largest
pirate ships. It had 52 guns on board.

## Parts of a ship

A ship's floor is called the deck.
Pirates worked on the deck.
They pulled ropes to move the
sails. Sails filled with wind and
pushed the ship through water.

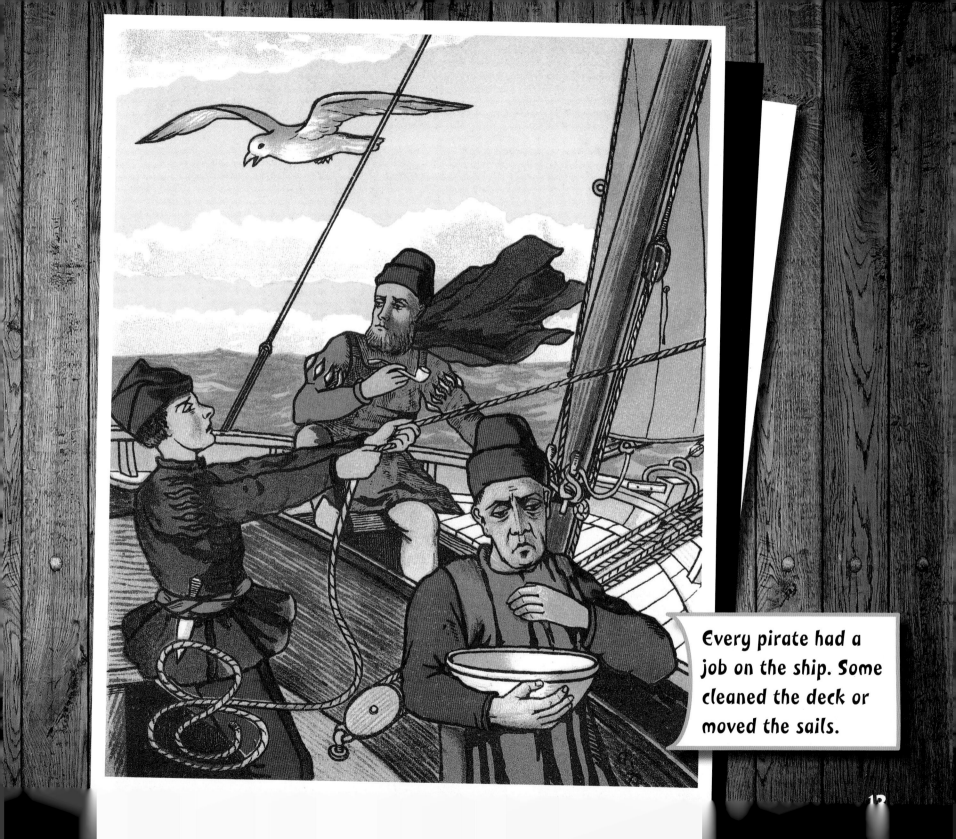

Every pirate had a job on the ship. Some cleaned the deck or moved the sails.

Pirates stored weapons and food in a room called the hold. Sometimes pirates made secret rooms in the hold to hide treasures.

Treasures such as gold and jewels were hidden in the hold.

## Ships in battle

Pirate ships looked scary.

Cannons lined the deck.

Pirate flags with painted bones

and skulls flapped in the wind.

cannons on
a ship

Battles could damage pirate ships. A damaged ship had to be mended quickly. Pirates risked being captured if their ships could not sail.

Pirates had to cover holes made by cannonballs and mend broken masts on ships.

## Pirate ships today

The Golden Age of Piracy is over. Today's pirates do not travel on ships with big sails and heavy cannons. But they still use small, fast boats to attack ships at sea.

modern pirates from Somalia, Africa

# Glossary

**attack** try to hurt someone or something

**cannon** heavy gun that fires large metal balls

**capture** take a person or place by force

**damage** harm done to something

**Golden Age of Piracy** period from 1690 to 1730, when thousands of people became pirates around the world

**pirate** person who steals from towns and ships

**raid** sudden, surprise attack

**shallow** not deep

**treasure** gold, jewels, money and other items of value

**warship** ship with many weapons, made for fighting wars at sea

# Books

*On a Pirate Ship,* Anna Milbourne and Benji Davies (Usborne Publishing, 2011)

*Pirate Ships* (See Inside), Rob Lloyd Jones (Usborne Publishing, 2007).

*Pirates* (Legends of the Sea), Rebecca Rissman (Raintree, 2011)

# Websites

**www.bbc.co.uk/cbeebies/swashbuckle-online/games**
Find the treasure and make the pirates walk the plank! Try these fun pirate games.

**www.jerseyheritage.org/learning/teacher-resources-pirates**
Do you know the difference between the mast and the crow's nest? Follow the links to colour and label a pirate ship, and make your own treasure map!

# Index